The Pocket Book of Positives

The Pocket Book of Positives

A reassuring companion for life's journey

ARCTURUS

ARCTURUS

This edition published in 2014 by Arcturus Publishing Limited
26/27 Bickels Yard, 151–153 Bermondsey Street,
London SE1 3HA

ISBN: 978-1-78212-867-0
AD004014NT

Printed in China

CONTENTS

CELEBRATING YOU

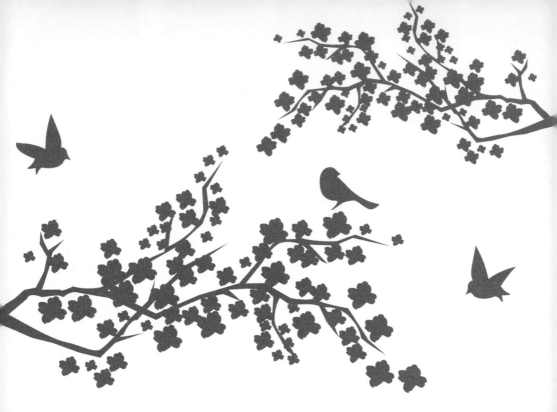

To love oneself is the beginning of a lifelong romance.

Oscar Wilde

> *Nobody can make you feel inferior without your consent.*
>
> Eleanor Roosevelt

Happiness is when you love who you are and you are able to accept yourself and others.

Bar Refaeli

I am never wrong when it comes to my own possibilities.

Placido Domingo

You don't have a soul. You are a soul. You have a body.

C.S. Lewis

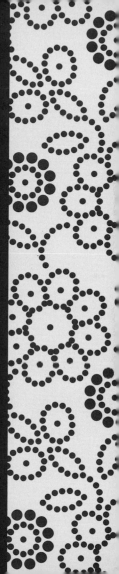

Your time is limited, so don't waste it living someone else's life.

Steve Jobs

When I let go
of what I am,
I become what
I might be.

Lao Tzu

Children learn more from what you are than what you teach.

W.E.B. DuBois

Find out what you like doing best and get someone to pay you for it.

Katharine Whitehorn

We are more interested in making others believe we are happy than in trying to be happy ourselves.

François de La Rochefoucauld

If you feel loved and cherished – even if it is only by yourself – then you will have more love to give to others, too.

Penelope Quest

A bird doesn't sing because it has an answer, it sings because it has a song.

Maya Angelou

May I be I is the only prayer – not may I be great or good or beautiful or wise or strong.

E.E. Cummings

No person is your friend who demands your silence, or denies your right to grow.

Alice Walker

Follow your inner moonlight; don't hide the madness.

Allen Ginsberg

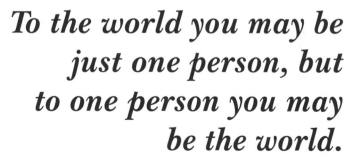

To the world you may be just one person, but to one person you may be the world.

Brandi Snyder

Lives are changed by a moment's listening to conscience, by a single and quiet inclination of the mind.

George A. Smith

It is not things in themselves that trouble us but our opinion of things.

Epictetus

Success is peace of mind, which is a direct result of self-satisfaction in knowing you made the effort to become the best of which you are capable.

John Wooden

Be independent of the good opinion of other people.

Abraham Harold Maslow

When we do the best we can, we never know what miracle is wrought in our life, or in the life of another.

Helen Keller

Serenity is knowing that your worst shot is still pretty good.

Johnny Miller

When a woman becomes her own best friend life is easier.

Diane von Furstenberg

Reputation is what men and women think of us; character is what God and angels know of us.

Thomas Paine

I am good, but not an angel. I do sin, but I am not the devil. I am just a small girl in a big world trying to find someone to love.

Marilyn Monroe

We are not what we know but what we are willing to learn.

Mary Catherine Bateson

The injunction that we should love our neighbors as ourselves means to us equally that we should love ourselves as we love our neighbors.

Barbara Deming

The only way to have a friend is to be one.

Ralph Waldo Emerson

Happiness is a matter of one's most ordinary and everyday mode of consciousness being busy and lively and unconcerned with self.

Iris Murdoch

Don't judge each day by the harvest
you reap, but by the seeds that
you plant.

Robert Louis Stevenson

**Learn to be quiet enough
to hear the genuine within
yourself so that you can hear
it in others.**

Marian Wright Edelman

The thing that is really hard, and really amazing, is giving up on being perfect and beginning the work of becoming yourself.

Anna Quindlen

Nobody really cares if you're miserable, so you might as well be happy.

Cynthia Nelms

What is happiness except the simple harmony between a man and the life he leads?

Albert Camus

Rest satisfied with doing well and leave others to talk of you as they will.

Pythagoras

We cannot do great things on this earth – only small things with great love.

Mother Teresa

The good ideas are all hammered out in agony by individuals, not spewed out by groups.

Charles Brower

There is no escape from you. The only way out is in.

Spike Milligan

I have tremendous faith in the universe. I feel at home on this planet. Even though it's a very big world out there, I plan on walking right through the middle of it unharmed.

Marion Ross

Don't be afraid to feel as angry or as loving as you can, because when you feel nothing, it's just death.

Lena Horne

I did what my conscience told me to do, and you can't fail if you do that.

Anita Hill

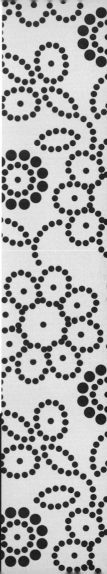

It takes a great deal of courage to stand up to your enemies, but even more to stand up to your friends.

J.K. Rowling

We can only be said to be alive in those moments when our hearts are conscious of our treasures.

Thornton Wilder

No matter what age you are, or what your circumstances might be, you are special, and you still have something unique to offer. Your life, because of who you are, has meaning.

Barbara De Angelis

One lives in the hope of becoming a memory.

Antonio Porchia

I have no regrets. I wouldn't have lived my life the way I did if I was going to worry about what people were going to say.

Ingrid Bergman

The first duty of a man is to think for himself.

José Martí

I would always rather be happy than dignified.

Charlotte Brontë

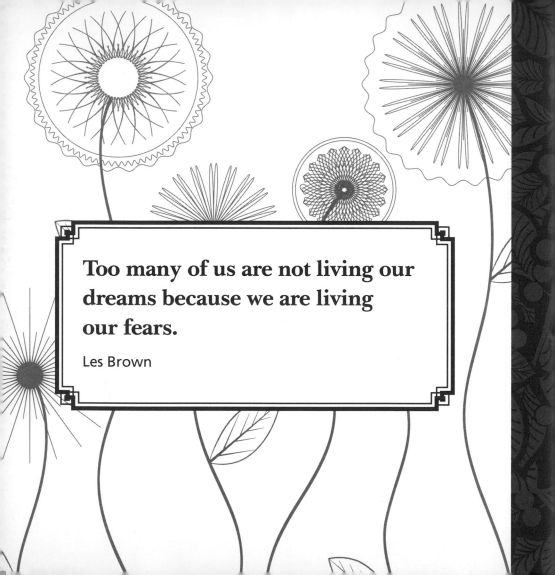

Too many of us are not living our dreams because we are living our fears.

Les Brown

There was never a genius without a tincture of madness.

Aristotle

Not being beautiful was the true blessing. Not being beautiful forced me to develop my inner resources. The pretty girl has a handicap to overcome.

Golda Meir

Just don't give up trying to do what you really want to do. Where there is love and inspiration, I don't think you can go wrong.

Ella Fitzgerald

Freedom discovers man the moment he loses concern over what impression he is making or about to make.

Bruce Lee

I don't want to be interesting. I want to be good.

Ludwig Mies van der Rohe

If you look into your own heart,
and you find nothing wrong
there, what is there to worry
about? What is there to fear?

Confucius

It's your place in the world; it's your life. Go on and do all you can with it, and make it the life you want to live.

Mae Jemison

There is a crack in everything. That's how the light gets in.

Leonard Cohen

I am in the world to change the world.

Käthe Kollwitz

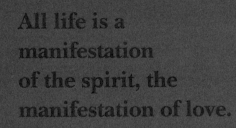

All life is a manifestation of the spirit, the manifestation of love.

Morihei Ueshiba

Don't try to figure out what other people want to hear from you; figure out what you have to say. It's the one and only thing you have to offer.

Barbara Kingsolver

It's only those who do nothing who make no mistakes.

Joseph Conrad

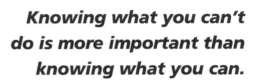

Knowing what you can't do is more important than knowing what you can.

Lucille Ball

Happiness is when what you think, what you say, and what you do are in harmony.

Mahatma Gandhi

Our best
thoughts
come
from
others.

Ralph Waldo Emerson

We know what
we are, but
know not what
we may be.

William Shakespeare

The important work of moving the world forward does not wait to be done by perfect men.

George Eliot

Two things you should never be angry at: what you can help and what you cannot help.

Thomas Fuller

A warm smile is the universal language of kindness.

William Arthur Ward

Virtue is the fount whence honour springs.

Christopher Marlowe

It's a rare person who wants to hear what he doesn't want to hear.

Dick Cavett

The main thing is to be moved, to love, to hope, to tremble, to live.

Auguste Rodin

Remember that the entire universe, with one trifling exception, is composed of others.

John Andrew Holmes

We don't laugh because we're happy – we're happy because we laugh.

William James

If you
want to be
happy, be.

Leo Tolstoy

Silences make the real conversations between friends. Not the saying but the never needing to say is what counts.

Margaret Lee Runbeck

Striving for excellence motivates you; striving for perfection is demoralizing.

Harriet Braiker

Hold fast to dreams
For if dreams die
Life is a broken-
winged bird
That cannot fly.

Langston Hughes

Hope is not a feeling or a mood or a personality type. Hope is a choice.

Jim Wallis

Your willingness to look at your darkness is what empowers you to change.

Iyanla Vanzant

You're only given a little spark of madness. You mustn't lose it.

Robin Williams

*When we ask
for advice, we are
usually looking for
an accomplice.*

Saul Bellow

**Imagination is more
important than knowledge.**

Albert Einstein

First keep peace
with yourself,
then you can
also bring peace
to others.

Thomas à Kempis

Those who are at war with others are not at peace with themselves.

William Hazlitt

A friend is a present you give yourself.

Robert Louis Stevenson

Life isn't about finding yourself. Life is about creating yourself.

George Bernard Shaw

Habit, if not resisted, soon becomes necessity.

Augustine of Hippo

When you would have a cordial for your spirits, think of the good qualities of your friends.

Marcus Aurelius

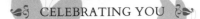

Be happy with what you have and are, be generous with both, and you won't have to hunt for happiness.

William E. Gladstone

POSITIVE CHANGE

Fortune favours the bold.

Terence

And the day came when the risk to remain tight in a bud was more painful than the risk it took to blossom.

Anaïs Nin

He has not learned the lesson of life who does not every day surmount a fear.

Ralph Waldo Emerson

The life you have led doesn't need to be the only life you have.

Anna Quindlen

We have to continually be jumping off cliffs and developing our wings on the way down.

Kurt Vonnegut

A ship is safe in the harbour, but that is not what ships are for.

William Greenough Thayer

The probability that we may fall in the struggle ought not to deter us from the support of a cause we believe to be just.

Abraham Lincoln

*Change is not merely necessary to life – it **is** life.*

Alvin Toffler

We must be willing to let go of the life we have planned, so as to have the life that is waiting for us.

E.M. Forster

It is right to be contented with what we have, but never with what we are.

James Mackintosh

The misfortunes hardest to bear are those which never happen.

James Russell Lowell

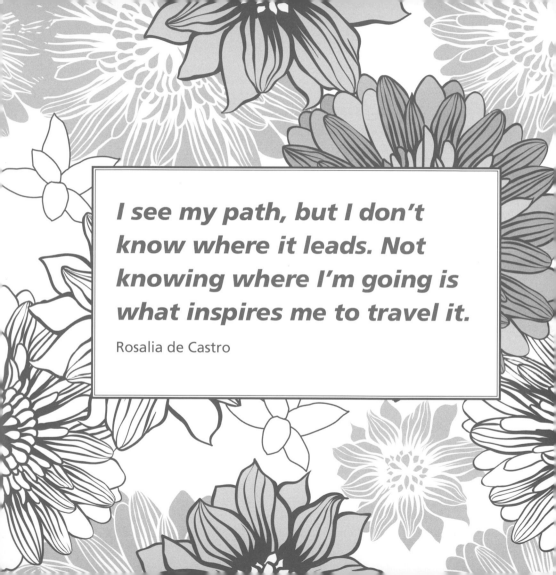

I see my path, but I don't know where it leads. Not knowing where I'm going is what inspires me to travel it.

Rosalia de Castro

Confusion is the beginning of wisdom.

Socrates

We don't have to engage in grand, heroic actions to participate in the process of change. Small acts, when multiplied by millions of people, can transform the world.

Howard Zinn

We must sail sometimes with the wind and sometimes against it — but we must sail, and not drift, nor lie at anchor.

Oliver Wendell Holmes, Jr.

Nought may endure but mutability.

Percy Bysshe Shelley

Stress is an ignorant state. It believes that everything is an emergency.

Natalie Goldberg

If you do not expect the unexpected you will not find it, for it is not to be reached by search or trail.

Heraclitus

Life's under no obligation to give us what we expect.

Margaret Mitchell

Happy people continuously change; and because they change they become more and more happy; and then more and more change is possible.

Osho

Change your thoughts and you change your world.

Norman Vincent Peale

I'm not afraid of storms, for I'm learning to sail my ship.

Louisa May Alcott

If we want things to stay as they are, things will have to change.

Giuseppe Tomasi di Lampedusa

At the height of laughter,
the universe is flung into
a kaleidoscope of new
possibilities.

Jean Houston

Luck affects everything; let your hook always be cast; in the stream where you least expect it, there will be a fish.

Ovid

Change is not made without inconvenience, even from worse to better.

Richard Hooker

Life is not measured by the number of breaths we take, but by the moments that take our breath away.

Maya Angelou

The more things you do, the more you can do.

Lucille Ball

If one does not know to which port one is sailing, no wind is favourable.

Seneca

You will find peace not by trying to escape your problems, but by confronting them courageously.

J. Donald Walters

I've found that luck is quite predictable. If you want more luck, take more chances. Be more active. Show up more often.

Brian Tracy

A woman's gifts will make room for her.

Hattie McDaniel

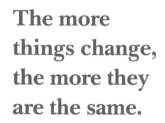

The more things change, the more they are the same.

Alphonse Karr

> *Luck is believing you're lucky.*
>
> Tennessee Williams

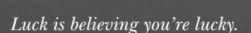

In giving advice, seek to help, not to please, your friend.

Solon

Nothing endures but change.

Heraclitus

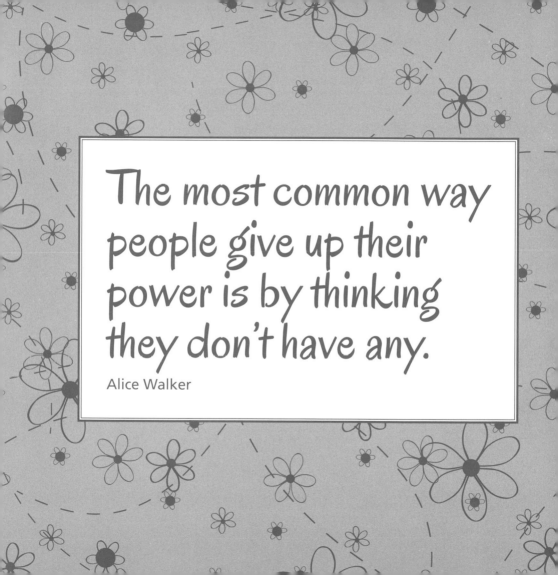

The most common way people give up their power is by thinking they don't have any.

Alice Walker

The only human institution which rejects progress is the cemetery.

Harold Wilson

Always go with the choice that scares you the most, because that's the one that is going to require the most from you.

Caroline Myss

There is nothing like a dream to create the future.

Victor Hugo

*Weep not that the world changes – did it keep
A stable, changeless state, it were cause indeed to weep.*

William Cullen Bryant

There is no learning to let go, or trying to let go. There is just letting go.

Lori Deschene

The question isn't who's going to let me; it's who's going to stop me?

Ayn Rand

If you want to control things in your life so bad, work on the mind. That's the only thing you should be trying to control.

Elizabeth Gilbert

The greatest gift is not being afraid to question.

Ruby Dee

> There is a tide in the affairs
>   of men,
> Which, taken at the flood,
>   leads on to fortune.

William Shakespeare

Nothing will ever be attempted
if all possible objections must
first be overcome.

Samuel Johnson

You have no security unless you can live bravely, excitingly, imaginatively; unless you can choose a challenge instead of competence.

Eleanor Roosevelt

You never lose by loving. You always lose by holding back.

Barbara De Angelis

When change itself can give no more,
'Tis easy to be true.

Sir Charles Sedley

**Courage leads to heaven;
fear, to death.**

Seneca

**To be fully alive, fully human,
and completely awake is to be
continually thrown out of the nest.**

Pema Chödrön

Throw your dreams into space like a kite, and you do not know what it will bring back: a new life, a new friend, a new love, a new country.

Anaïs Nin

Stop wearing your wishbone where your backbone ought to be.

Elizabeth Gilbert

Take chances, make mistakes. That's how you grow. Pain nourishes your courage. You have to fail in order to practice being brave.

Mary Tyler Moore

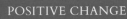

Giving frees us from the familiar territory of our own needs by opening our mind to the unexplained worlds occupied by the needs of others.

Barbara Bush

All things must change
To something new, to something strange

Henry Wadsworth Longfellow

Courage is like a muscle. We strengthen it by use.

Ruth Gordon

As for the future, your task is not
to foresee it but to enable it.

Antoine de Saint-Exupéry

Women are never stronger than when they arm themselves with their weaknesses.

Madame Marie du Deffand

You may be disappointed if you fail, but you are doomed if you don't try.

Beverly Sills

Because things are the way they are, things will not stay the way they are.

Bertolt Brecht

Nothing in life is to be feared. It is only to be understood.

Marie Curie

You cannot find peace by avoiding life.

Virginia Woolf

Destiny is a name often given in retrospect to choices that had dramatic consequences.

J.K. Rowling

I am a writer who came from a sheltered life. A sheltered life can be daring as well. For all serious daring starts from within.

Eudora Welty

The universe is change; our life is what our thoughts make it.

Marcus Aurelius

Life begins at the end of your comfort zone.

Neale Donald Walsch

As we are liberated from our own fear, our presence automatically liberates others.

Marianne Williamson

Adventure without risk is Disneyland.

Doug Coupland

Opportunity dances with those who are already on the dance floor.

H. Jackson Brown Jr.

Life shrinks or expands in proportion to one's courage.

Anaïs Nin

One of the most courageous things you can do is identify yourself, know who you are, what you believe in and where you want to go.

Sheila Murray Bethel

You take your life in your own hands, and what happens? A terrible thing, no one to blame.

Erica Jong

A little rebellion now and then is a good thing.

Thomas Jefferson

We must believe that we are gifted for something, and that this thing, at whatever cost, must be attained.

Marie Curie

Either life entails courage, or it ceases to be life.

E.M. Forster

Live your life from your heart. Share from your heart. And your story will touch and heal people's souls.

Melody Beattie

Love is what we were born with. Fear is what we learned here.

Marianne Williamson

We have it in our power to begin the world over again.

Thomas Paine

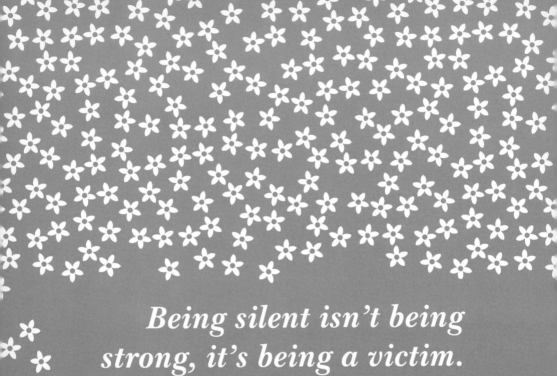

Being silent isn't being strong, it's being a victim.

Jane Powell

> **Do not go where the path may lead, go instead where there is no path and leave a trail.**
>
> Ralph Waldo Emerson

I have learned over the years that when one's mind is made up, this diminishes fear; knowing what must be done does away with fear.

Rosa Parks

There is a fuel in us which needs to be ignited with sparks.

Johann Gottfried von Herder

You move totally away from reality when you believe that there is a legitimate reason to suffer.

Byron Katie

Our worst misfortunes
never happen, and
most miseries lie in
anticipation.

Honoré de Balzac

Quiet minds cannot be perplexed or frightened, but go on in fortune or misfortune at their own private pace, like a clock during a thunderstorm.

Robert Louis Stevenson

Never be afraid to fall apart, because it is an opportunity to rebuild yourself the way you wish you had been all along.

Rae Smith

Optimism is true moral courage.

Ernest Shackleton

Understand that the right to choose your path is a sacred privilege. Use it. Dwell in possibility.

Oprah Winfrey

The world is a
book, and those
who do not travel
read only a page.

Saint Augustine

The trouble with life isn't that there is no answer, it's that there are so many answers.

Ruth Fulton Benedict

Avoiding danger is no safer in the long run than outright exposure. The fearful are caught as often as the bold.

Helen Keller

Go and make interesting mistakes, make amazing mistakes, make glorious and fantastic mistakes. Break rules. Leave the world more interesting for your being here.

Neil Gaiman

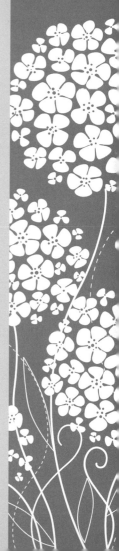

He who awaits much can
expect little.

Gabriel García Márquez

Change is the law of
life. And those who
look only to the past
or present are certain
to miss the future.

John F. Kennedy

To go forward is
to move toward
perfection.
March on, and
fear not the
thorns, or the
sharp stones
on life's path.

Khalil Gibran

A good traveller
has no fixed plans,
and is not intent
on arriving.

Lao Tzu

When I dare to be powerful – to use my strength in the service of my vision, then it becomes less and less important whether I am afraid.

Audre Lorde

A goal without a plan is just a wish.

Antoine de Saint-Exupéry

No matter who you are, no matter what you did, no matter where you've come from, you can always change, become a better version of yourself.

Madonna

LIFE'S SIMPLE PLEASURES

Find ecstasy in life; the mere sense of living is joy enough.

Emily Dickinson

There must be quite
a few things that a
hot bath won't cure,
but I don't know
many of them.

Sylvia Plath

To awaken quite alone in a strange town is one of the pleasantest sensations in the world.

Freya Stark

If people sat outside and looked at the stars each night, I'll bet they'd live a lot differently.

Bill Watterson

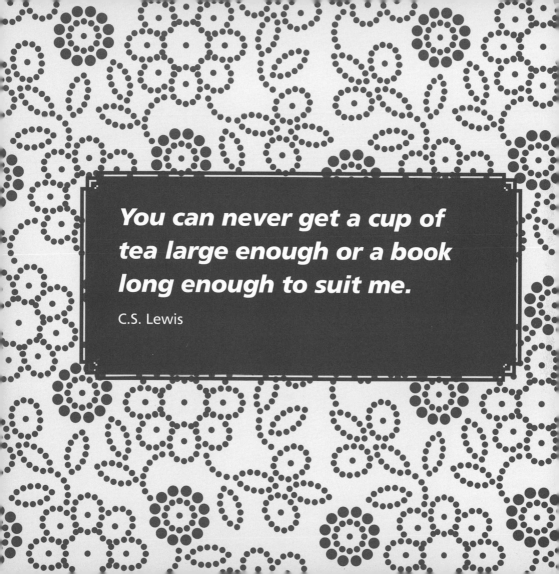

You can never get a cup of tea large enough or a book long enough to suit me.

C.S. Lewis

Most people don't allow the happy moment, because they're so busy trying to get a happy life.

Esther Hicks

There is no need to go to India or anywhere else to find peace. You will find that deep place of silence right in your room, your garden or even your bathtub.

Elisabeth Kübler-Ross

There is no friend as loyal as a book.

Ernest Hemingway

Don't underestimate the value of Doing Nothing, of just going along, listening to all the things you can't hear, and not bothering.

A.A. Milne

All you need in the world is love and laughter. That's all anybody needs. To have love in one hand and laughter in the other.

August Wilson

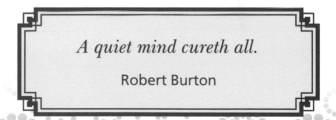

A quiet mind cureth all.

Robert Burton

If you want to know what God thinks of money, just look at the people he gave it to.

Dorothy Parker

Laughter is an instant vacation.

Milton Berle

The only man who is really free is the one who can turn down an invitation to dinner without giving an excuse.

Jules Renard

Research is what I'm doing when I don't know what I'm doing.

Wernher von Braun

The trouble with having an open mind, of course, is that people will insist on coming along and trying to put things in it.

Terry Pratchett

I like work: it fascinates me. I can sit and look at it for hours.

Jerome K. Jerome

The trouble with the rat-race is that even if you win, you're still a rat.

Lily Tomlin

There's one good thing about snow, it makes your lawn look as nice as your neighbor's.

Clyde Moore

Some folks can look
so busy doing nothing
that they seem
indispensable.

Kin Hubbard

Some people feel the rain – others just get wet.

Roger Miller

Outside of a dog, a book is man's best friend. Inside of a dog it's too dark to read.

Groucho Marx

The world is full of magical things patiently waiting for our wits to grow sharper.

Bertrand Russell

My mother says I didn't open my eyes for eight days after I was born, but when I did the first thing I saw was an engagement ring. I was hooked.

Elizabeth Taylor

My mind's my kingdom.

Francis Quarles

Look at the trees, look at the birds, look at the clouds, look at the stars . . . and if you have eyes you will be able to see that the whole existence is joyful . . . Look at the flowers – for no reason. It is simply unbelievable how happy flowers are.

Osho

Silence is more
musical than any song.

Christina Rossetti

**Pleasures newly found are sweet
When they lie about our feet.**

William Wordsworth

To sit with a dog on a hillside on a glorious afternoon is to be back in Eden, where doing nothing was not boring — it was peace.

Milan Kundera

I travel not to go anywhere, but to go. I travel for travel's sake. The great affair is to move.

Robert Louis Stevenson

When I go out into the countryside and see the sun and the green and everything flowering, I say to myself, yes indeed, all that belongs to me!

Henri Rousseau

I love that quiet time when nobody's up and the animals are all happy to see me.

Olivia Newton-John

As I get older I notice the years less and the seasons more.

John Hubbard

Give plenty of what is given to you, and listen to pity's call; don't think the little you give is great and the much you get is small.

Phoebe Cary

There are no rules of architecture for a castle in the clouds.

G.K. Chesterton

My advice to you is not to inquire why or whither, but just enjoy your ice-cream while it's on your plate.

Thornton Wilder

One child, one teacher, one pen and one book can change the world.

Malala Yousafzai

I long for rural and domestic scenes, for the warbling of birds and the prattling of my children.

John Adams

Thank God men cannot fly, and lay waste the sky as well as the earth.

Henry David Thoreau

The ideal of calm exists in a sitting cat.

Jules Renard

Arranging a bowl of flowers in the morning can give a sense of quiet in a crowded day – like writing a poem or saying a prayer.

Anne Morrow Lindbergh

How strange that Nature does not knock, and yet does not intrude!

Emily Dickinson

What a lovely surprise to finally discover how unlonely being alone can be.

Ellen Burstyn

Sometimes when we are generous in small, barely detectable ways it can change someone else's life forever.

Margaret Cho

How glorious a greeting the sun gives the mountains!

John Muir

We all live under the same sky, but we don't all have the same horizon.

Konrad Adenauer

Humility is not thinking less of yourself, it's thinking of yourself less.

C.S. Lewis

To sit in the shade on a fine day and look upon verdure is the most perfect refreshment.

Jane Austen

Never does nature say one thing and wisdom another.

Juvenal

Laughter is the closest distance between two people.

Victor Borge

The search for happiness is one of the chief sources of unhappiness.

Eric Hoffer

You can't live a perfect day without doing something for someone who will never be able to repay you.

Debbie Macomber

I have learned to seek my happiness by limiting my desires, rather than in attempting to satisfy them.

John Stuart Mill

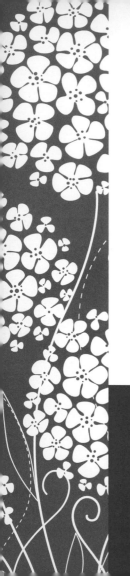

Great things are done when men and mountains meet. This is not done by jostling in the street.

William Blake

Always laugh when you can. It is cheap medicine.

Lord Byron

Nobody sees a flower really, it is so small. We haven't time, and to see takes time – like to have a friend takes time.

Georgia O'Keeffe

Peace is the result of retraining your mind to process life as it is, rather than as you think it should be.

Wayne W. Dyer

The soul's joy lies in doing.

Percy Bysshe Shelley

We usually find that it is the simplest things – not the great occasions – that in retrospect give off the greatest glow of happiness.

Bob Hope

The human soul needs actual beauty more than bread.

D.H. Lawrence

One touch of nature makes the whole world kin.

William Shakespeare

Peace is when
time doesn't
matter as it
passes by.

Maria Schell

Half an hour's
meditation each
day is essential,
except when you
are busy. Then
a full hour is
needed.

St Francis de Sales

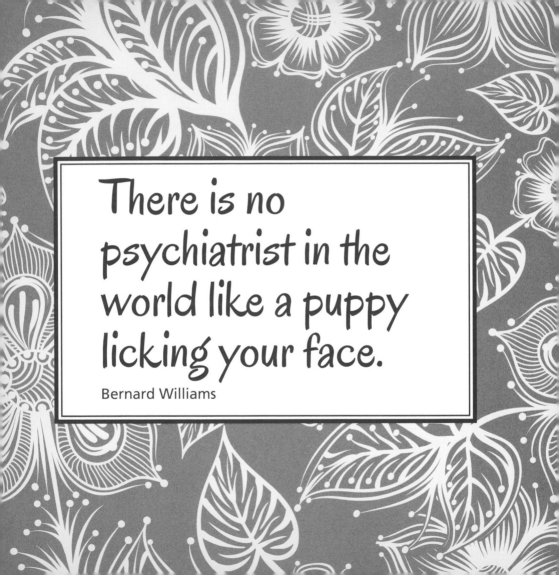

There is no psychiatrist in the world like a puppy licking your face.

Bernard Williams

Wellbeing is attained by little and little, and nevertheless is no little thing.

Zeno

Everything has beauty, but not everyone sees it.

Confucius

Animals are such agreeable friends, they ask no questions, they pass no criticisms.

George Eliot

Happiness always looks small when you hold it in your hands, but let it go and you learn at once how big and precious it is.

Maxim Gorky

I'm a girl that likes the storms. I love feeling alive, I love walking out in the cold in my bare feet and feeling the ice on my toes.

Tori Amos

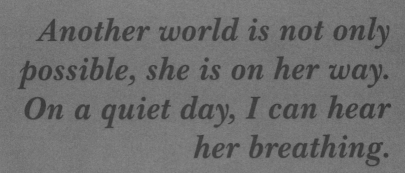

Another world is not only possible, she is on her way. On a quiet day, I can hear her breathing.

Arundhati Roy

A kind word is never thrown away.

Sir Arthur Helps

Wisdom begins in wonder.

Socrates

There are short cuts to happiness, and dancing is one of them.

Vicki Baum

In great moments life seems neither right nor wrong, but something greater: it seems inevitable.

Margaret Sherwood

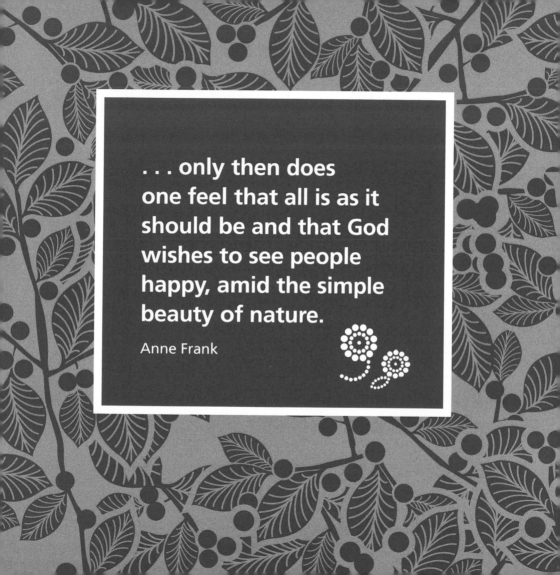

. . . only then does
one feel that all is as it
should be and that God
wishes to see people
happy, amid the simple
beauty of nature.

Anne Frank

Wandering re-establishes the original harmony which once existed between man and the universe.

Anatole France

It is only possible to live happily ever after on a day-to-day basis.

Margaret Bonnano

You are a child of the universe no less than the trees and the stars; you have a right to be here.

Max Ehrmann

The time you enjoy wasting is not wasted time.

John Lennon

Children think not of what is past, nor what is to come, but enjoy the present time, which few of us do.

Jean de La Bruyère

A thing of beauty is a joy for ever.

John Keats

Nothing is more beautiful than the loveliness of the woods before sunrise.

George Washington Carver

The very existence of libraries affords the best evidence that we may yet have hope for the future of man.

T.S. Eliot

Birds sing after a storm; why shouldn't people feel as free to delight in whatever remains to them?

Rose Kennedy

Nothing is more useful than silence.

Menander of Athens

It is only in the country that we can get to know a person or a book.

Cyril Connolly

All you need is love. But a little chocolate now and then doesn't hurt.

Charles M. Schulz

There are always flowers for those who want to see them.

Henri Matisse

The happiness of life is made up of minute fractions – the little, soon forgotten charities of a kiss or a smile, a kind look or heartfelt compliment.

Samuel Taylor Coleridge

Great opportunities to help others seldom come, but small ones surround us daily.

Sally Koch

It is neither wealth nor splendor, but tranquility and occupation which bring one happiness.

Thomas Jefferson

Happiness never lays its finger on its pulse.

Adam Smith

Sometimes the most important thing in a whole day is the rest we take between two deep breaths.

Etty Hillesum

I long to accomplish a great and noble task; but my chief duty is to accomplish small tasks as if they were great and noble.

Helen Keller

This moment contains all moments.

C.S. Lewis

I believe that if one always looked at the skies, one would end up with wings.

Gustave Flaubert

Those who dwell among the beauties and mysteries of the earth are never alone or weary of life.

Rachel Carson

There is nothing in the world more peaceful than apple-leaves with an early moon.

Alice Meynell

All who would win joy must share it; happiness was born a twin.

Lord Byron

It is the nature of the wise to resist pleasures, but the foolish to be a slave to them.

Epictetus

THE GREAT
AND THE GOOD

Voyage, travel, and change of place impart vigour.

Seneca

In matters of conscience, first thoughts are best. In matters of prudence, last thoughts are best.

Robert Hall

Strength does not come from physical capacity. It comes from an indomitable will.

Mahatma Gandhi

There are still many causes worth sacrificing for, so much history yet to be made.

Michelle Obama

Never confuse movement with action.

Ernest Hemingway

Where there is no hope, it is incumbent on us to invent it.

Albert Camus

Don't wait around for other people to be happy for you. Any happiness you get you've got to make yourself.

Alice Walker

Age is no barrier. It's a limitation you put on your mind.

Jackie Joyner-Kersee

Do what you can,
with what you have,
where you are.

Eleanor Roosevelt

All we need to make us really happy is something to be enthusiastic about.

Charles Kingsley

The key to success is to risk thinking unconventional thoughts.

Trevor Baylis

I've learned that people will forget what you said, people will forget what you did, but people will never forget how you made them feel.

Maya Angelou

Each person must live their life as a model for others.

Rosa Parks

Nature reserves the right to inflict upon her children the most terrifying jests.

Thornton Wilder

Be slow to fall into friendship; but when thou art in, continue firm and constant.

Socrates

A champion is afraid of losing. Everyone else is afraid of winning.

Billie Jean King

We do not judge the people we love.

Jean-Paul Sartre

Think in the morning. Act in the noon. Eat in the evening. Sleep in the night.

William Blake

One resolution I have made, and try always to keep, is this: 'To rise above little things.'

John Burroughs

Laughter is the sensation of feeling good all over and showing it principally in one place.

Josh Billings

The meaning of life is to find your gift, the purpose of life is to give it away.

Joy J. Golliver

I believe in the impossible because no one else does.

Florence Griffith Joyner

Action may not always bring happiness; but there is no happiness without action.

Benjamin Disraeli

The bird of paradise alights only on the hand that does not grasp.

John Berry

When you reduce life to black and white, you never see rainbows.

Rachel Houston

A cup that is already full cannot have more added to it. In order to receive the further good to which we are entitled, we must give of that which we have.

Margaret Becker

The philosophers have only interpreted the world, in various ways; the point is to change it.

Karl Marx

Discovery consists not in seeking new lands, but in seeing with new eyes.

Marcel Proust

The art of creation is older than the art of killing.

Andrei Voznesensky

Against the assault of laughter nothing can stand.

Mark Twain

Life is very short and what we have to do must be done in the now.

Audre Lorde

No matter what accomplishments you make, somebody helped you.

Althea Gibson

Surround yourself with only people who are going to lift you higher.

Oprah Winfrey

We are not held back by the love we
didn't receive in the past, but by the
love we're not extending in the present.

Marianne Williamson

Each man is the architect of his own fate.

Appius Claudius

I have found the paradox that if I love until it hurts, then there is no hurt, but only more love.

Mother Teresa

You begin saving the world by saving one person at a time.

Charles Bukowski

The kind of beauty I want most is the hard-to-get kind that comes from within – strength, courage, dignity.

Ruby Dee

The constant happiness is curiosity.

Alice Munro

To travel is to take a journey into yourself.

Danny Kaye

There is only one rule for being a good talker – learn to listen.

Christopher Morley

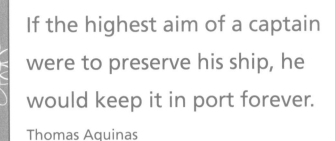

If the highest aim of a captain were to preserve his ship, he would keep it in port forever.

Thomas Aquinas

Style is knowing who you are, what you want to say, and not giving a damn.

Gore Vidal

I don't want to get to the end of my life and find that I lived just the length of it. I want to have lived the width of it as well.

Diane Ackerman

Keep your face always toward the sunshine – and shadows will fall behind you.

Walt Whitman

Taking joy in living is a woman's best cosmetic.

Rosalind Russell

The man who has no imagination has no wings.

Muhammad Ali

Friendship improves happiness and abates misery by the doubling of our joy and the dividing of our grief.

Marcus Cicero

We think more
of extending life
than of filling it.

Tomas Masaryk

Talent is God-given.
Be humble. Fame is
man-given. Be grateful.
Conceit is self-given.
Be careful.

John Wooden

I have found that among
its other benefits, giving
liberates the soul of
the giver.

Maya Angelou

Joyfulness keeps the heart and face young. A good laugh makes us better friends with ourselves and everybody around us.

Orison Swett Marden

The hand is the cutting edge of the mind.

Jacob Bronowski

Pessimism becomes a self-fulfilling prophecy; it reproduces itself by crippling our willingness to act.

Howard Zinn

Call no man foe, but never love a stranger.

Stella Benson

I am an optimist. It does not seem to be much use being anything else.

Winston Churchill

> Give, if it means to suffer; give, if it means to lose; give, in life; give, in death; give forever throughout eternity.

Evangeline Cory Booth

Whatever the mind of man can conceive and believe, it can achieve.

Napoleon Hill

Once you have achieved a state of happiness, you must never become lax about maintaining it.

Elizabeth Gilbert

To thine own self be true.

William Shakespeare

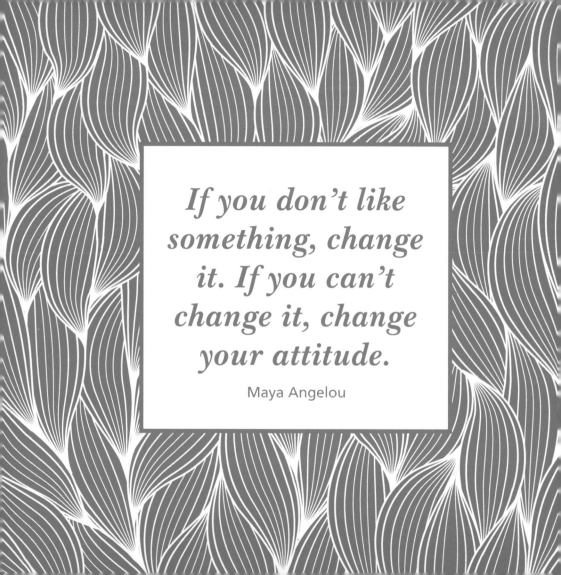

If you don't like something, change it. If you can't change it, change your attitude.

Maya Angelou

If there is to be any peace it will come through being, not having.

Henry Miller

Give light and people will find the way.

Ella Baker

Truth is a deep kindness that teaches us to be content in our everyday life and share with other people the same happiness.

Khalil Gibran

If it is not right,
do not do it; if
it is not true,
do not say it.

Marcus Aurelius

The love we give away is the only love we keep.

Elbert Hubbard

Do not care how many, but whom, you please.

Syrus

Use your head, but follow your heart.

Dame Nancy Rothwell

Act as if what you do makes a difference. It does.

William James

> *What we have done for ourselves alone dies with us.*
>
> Albert Pike

Kindness, I've discovered, is everything in life.

Isaac Bashevis Singer

Above all, you must fight conceit, envy, and every kind of ill-feeling in your heart.

Abraham Cahan

If truth doesn't set you free, generosity of spirit will.

Katerina Stoykova Klemer

Go confidently in the direction of your dreams.

Henry David Thoreau

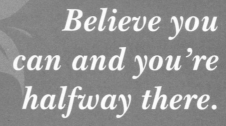

Believe you can and you're halfway there.

Theodore Roosevelt

My courage always rises at every attempt to intimidate me.

Jane Austen

Fantasy is a necessary ingredient in living, it's a way of looking at life through the wrong end of a telescope. Which is what I do, and that enables you to laugh at life's realities.

Dr Seuss

For small creatures such as
we the vastness is bearable
only through love.

Carl Sagan

People who believe in miracles do not make much fuss when they actually encounter one.

Alice Munro

If honour were profitable, everybody would be honourable.

Thomas More

Dreaming, after all, is a form of planning.

Gloria Steinem

Live, travel, adventure, bless, and don't be sorry.

Jack Kerouac

Gratitude makes sense of our past, brings peace for today, and creates a vision for tomorrow.

Melody Beattie

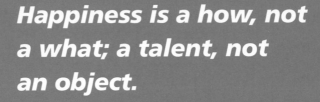

Happiness is a how, not a what; a talent, not an object.

Hermann Hesse

Take care of all your memories, for you cannot relive them.

Bob Dylan

You don't get to choose how you're going to die, or when. You can only decide how you're going to live now.

Joan Baez

The shoe that fits one person pinches another; there is no recipe for living that suits all cases.

Carl Jung

If a thing is worth doing, it is worth doing slowly . . . very slowly.

Gypsy Rose Lee

One of the greatest problems of our time is that many are schooled, but few are educated.

Thomas More

The only critic is a full house.

Rudolf Nureyev

You are never too old to set another goal or to dream a new dream.

C.S. Lewis

Nobody made a greater mistake than he who did nothing because he could only do a little.

Edmund Burke

Kindness is a language which the deaf can hear and the blind can see.

Mark Twain

Stop worrying about the potholes in the road and celebrate the journey.

Fitzhugh Mullan

There is no such thing as darkness, only a failure to see.

Malcolm Muggeridge

You have to find what's good and true and beautiful in your life as it is now.

Mitch Albom

Wars begin in the minds of men, and in those minds, love and compassion would have built the defences of peace.

U Thant

You will never 'find' time for anything. If you want time, you must make it.

Charles Buxton

Never look down on anybody unless you're helping them up.

Reverend Jesse Jackson

Start with what is right rather than what is acceptable.

Franz Kafka

Life is either a daring adventure or nothing.

Helen Keller

The voice of conscience is so delicate that it is easy to stifle it; but it is also so clear that it is impossible to mistake it.

Madame de Staël

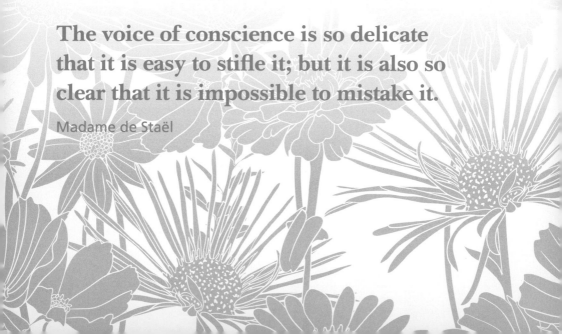

You cannot protect yourself from sadness without protecting yourself from happiness.

Jonathan Safran Foer

Blessed is he who expects nothing, for he shall never be disappointed.

Alexander Pope

A woman's guess is much more accurate than a man's certainty.

Rudyard Kipling

SILVER LININGS

When something seems to go wrong, it's invariably part of a larger right.

Jed McKenna

Laugh, and the world laughs with you
Weep, and you weep alone.
For the sad old earth must borrow its mirth
But has trouble enough of its own.

Ella Wheeler Wilcox

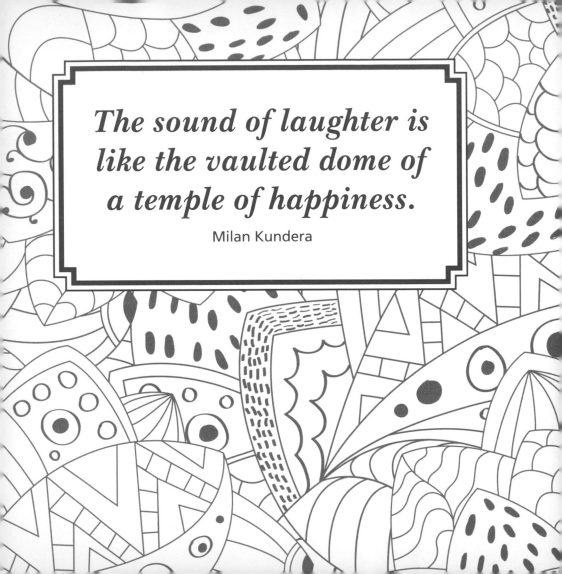

The sound of laughter is like the vaulted dome of a temple of happiness.

Milan Kundera

There is always a little more toothpaste in the tube. Think about it.

Bill Bryson

That which does not defeat me makes me stronger.

Friedrich Nietzsche

*There is nothing in the world
so much admired as a man
who knows how to bear
unhappiness with courage.*

Seneca

Where life is more
terrible than death,
it is then the truest
valour to dare
to live.

Sir Thomas Browne

There's always
something to suggest
that you'll never be
who you wanted to be.
Your choice is
to take it or keep
on moving.

Phylicia Rashad

> All life's battles teach us something,
> even those we lose.
>
> Paulo Coelho

You have to count on living every single day in a way you believe will make you feel good about your life – so that if it were over tomorrow, you'd be content with yourself.

Jane Seymour

We are all in the gutter, but some of us are looking at the stars.

Oscar Wilde

Life will always be sorrowful. We can't change it, but we can change our attitude toward it.

Joseph Campbell

*Life is mainly froth and
    bubble
Two things stand like stone –
Kindness in another's trouble,
Courage in your own.*

Adam Gordon

*Life is 10 percent what you
make it, and 90 percent how
you take it.*

Irving Berlin

I think laughter may be a form of courage. As humans we sometimes stand tall and look into the sun and laugh, and I think we are never more brave than when we do that.

Linda Ellerbee

Whatever chance shall bring, we will bear with equanimity.

Terence

Every exit is an entry somewhere else.

Tom Stoppard

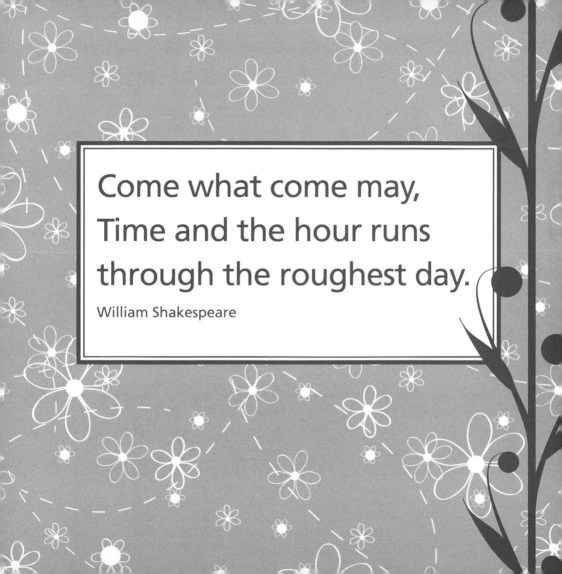

Come what come may,
Time and the hour runs
through the roughest day.

William Shakespeare

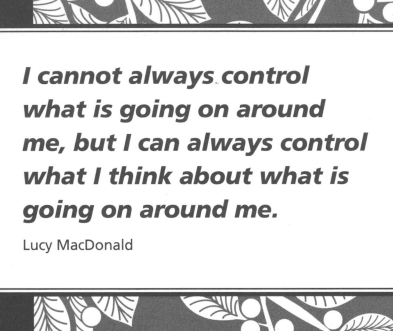

I cannot always control what is going on around me, but I can always control what I think about what is going on around me.

Lucy MacDonald

Ill fortune never crushed that man whom good fortune deceived not.

Francis Bacon

Gird your hearts with silent fortitude, suffering, yet hoping all things.

Felicia Hemans

The true way to soften one's troubles is to solace those of others.

Madame de Maintenon

Mixing humour and harsh reality is a very human behaviour, it's the way people stay sane in their daily lives.

Jorge García

Mortals grow swiftly in misfortune.

Hesiod

Life may change, but
   it may fly not;
Hope may vanish, but
   can die not;
Truth be veiled,
   but still it burneth;
Love repulsed, but
   it returneth.

Percy Bysshe Shelley

The pessimist complains about the wind; the optimist expects it to change; the realist adjusts the sails.

William Arthur Ward

The human race has one really effective weapon, and that is laughter.

Mark Twain

An act of love, a voluntary taking on oneself of some of the pain of the world, increases the courage and love and hope of all.

Dorothy Day

Here is a rule to remember in future, when anything tempts you to be bitter: not 'This is misfortune', but 'To bear this worthily is good fortune.'

Marcus Aurelius

The pain I feel now is the happiness I had before. That's the deal.

C.S. Lewis

Laughter and tears are both responses to frustration and exhaustion. I myself prefer to laugh, since there is less cleaning up to do afterward.

Kurt Vonnegut

I'm so glad I never feel important; it does complicate life!

Eleanor Roosevelt

The thing that makes you exceptional, if you are at all, is inevitably that which must also make you lonely.

Lorraine Hansberry

Men stumble over pebbles, never over mountains.

Marilyn French

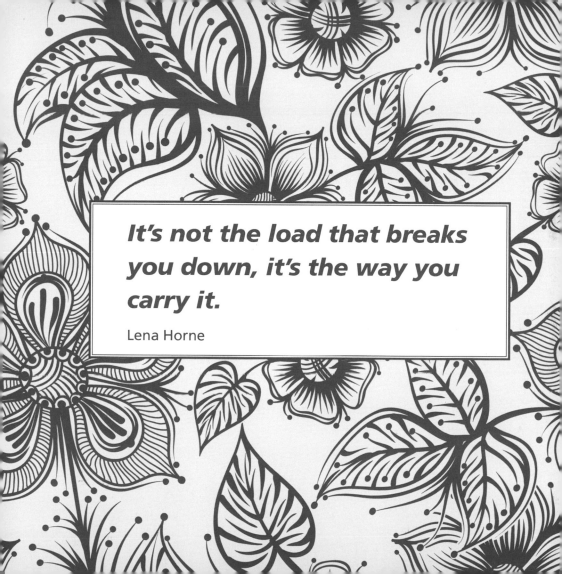

It's not the load that breaks you down, it's the way you carry it.

Lena Horne

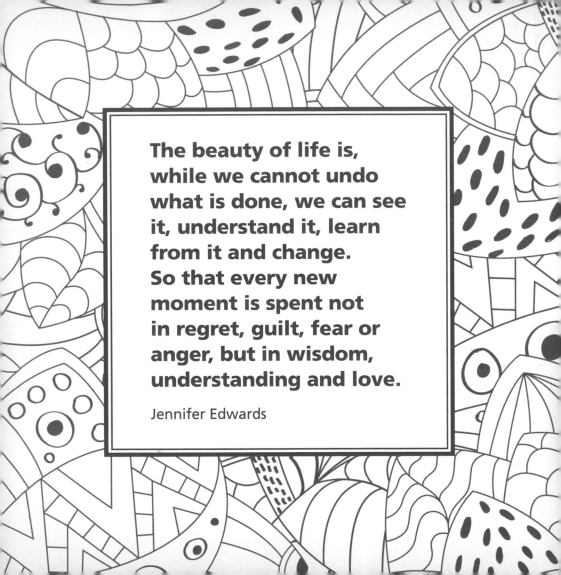

The beauty of life is,
while we cannot undo
what is done, we can see
it, understand it, learn
from it and change.
So that every new
moment is spent not
in regret, guilt, fear or
anger, but in wisdom,
understanding and love.

Jennifer Edwards

The best thing one can do when it's raining is to let it rain.

Henry Wadsworth Longfellow

The best way to cheer yourself up is to try to cheer somebody else up.

Mark Twain

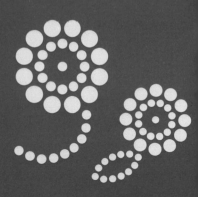

There's no life
without humor.
It can make
the wonderful
moments of life
truly glorious,
and it can make
tragic moments
bearable.

Rufus Wainwright

Measure thy life by loss instead of gain; not by the wine drunk, but by the wine poured forth.

Harriet King

Remember that what you now have was once among the things you only hoped for.

Epicurus

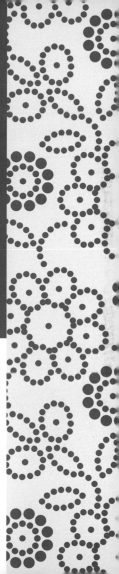

If you can't make it better, you can laugh at it.

Erma Bombeck

Anything that is created must sooner or later die. Enlightenment is permanent because we have not produced it; we have merely discovered it.

Chogyam Trungpa

There are two ways of meeting difficulties. You alter the difficulties or you alter yourself to meet them.

Phyllis Bottome

Restlessness and discontent are the necessities of progress.

Thomas Edison

This is a good sign, having a broken heart. It means we have tried for something.

Elizabeth Gilbert

A true friend never gets in your way unless you happen to be going down.

Arnold H. Glasow

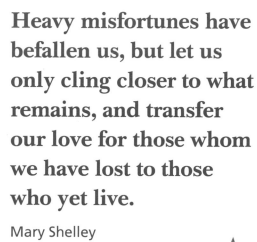

Heavy misfortunes have befallen us, but let us only cling closer to what remains, and transfer our love for those whom we have lost to those who yet live.

Mary Shelley

Life is thickly sown with thorns, and I know no other remedy than to pass quickly through them. The longer we dwell on our misfortunes, the greater is their power to harm us.

Voltaire

Everything flows and nothing abides.

Heraclitus

The word 'happy' would lose its meaning if it were not balanced by sadness.

Carl Jung

Laughter gives us distance. It allows us to step back from an event, deal with it and then move on.

Bob Newhart

There are two ways of spreading light: to be the candle or the mirror that reflects it.

Edith Wharton

If we will be quiet and ready enough, we shall find compensation in every disappointment.

Henry David Thoreau

Remember that
sometimes not
getting what
you want is
a wonderful
stroke of luck.

Tenzin Gyatso, 14th Dalai Lama

What you think, you become.

Buddha

If there were no difficulties there would be no success; if there were nothing to struggle for, there would be nothing to be achieved.

Samuel Smiles

Laughter can help relieve tension in even the heaviest of matters.

Allen Klein

If you surrender to the wind, you can ride it.

Toni Morrison

Some people go to priests; others to poetry; I to my friends.

Virginia Woolf

Everything
that irritates us
about others can
lead us to an
understanding
of ourselves.

Carl Jung

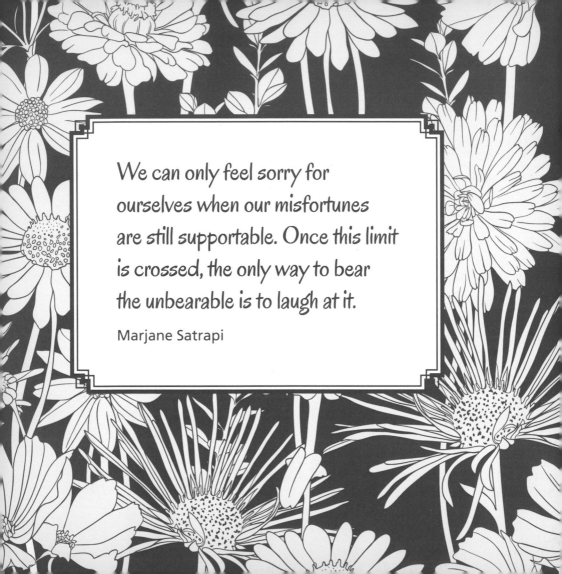

We can only feel sorry for ourselves when our misfortunes are still supportable. Once this limit is crossed, the only way to bear the unbearable is to laugh at it.

Marjane Satrapi

The greater part of our happiness or misery depends on our dispositions and not our circumstances.

Martha Washington

So many tangles in life are ultimately hopeless that we have no appropriate sword other than laughter.

Gordon W. Allport

In everyone's life,
at some time, our
inner fire goes out.
It is then burst into
flame by an encounter
with another human
being. We should all
be thankful for those
people who rekindle
the inner spirit.

Albert Schweitzer

Things turn out best for the people who make the best out of the way things turn out.

Art Linkletter

The art of love is largely the art of persistence.

Albert Ellis

We must accept finite disappointment, but never lose infinite hope.

Martin Luther King Jr.

Life is full of misery, loneliness and suffering – and it's all over much too soon.

Woody Allen

Laughter makes you live better and longer.

Gail Parent

Holding on to anger, resentment and hurt only gives you tense muscles, a headache and a sore jaw from clenching your teeth.

Joan Lunden

*We all look.
The lucky
find. The
wise accept.*

Nora Roberts

Two men look out through
the same bars; one sees the
mud and one sees the stars.

Frederick Langbridge

If we had no winter, the spring would not be so pleasant: if we did not sometimes taste of adversity, prosperity would not be so welcome.

Anne Bradstreet

One's life has value so long as one attributes value to the life of others, by means of love, friendship, and compassion.

Simone de Beauvoir

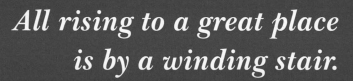

All rising to a great place is by a winding stair.

Francis Bacon

I know God will not give me anything I can't handle. I just wish that He didn't trust me so much.

Mother Teresa

Every conquering temptation represents a new fund of moral energy. Every trial endured and weathered in the right spirit makes a soul nobler and stronger than it was before.

W.B. Yeats

No pessimist ever discovered the secrets of the stars, or sailed to uncharted land, or opened a new heaven to the human spirit.

Helen Keller

If the skies fall, one may hope to catch larks.

François Rabelais

Laughter is the sun
that drives winter
from the human face.

Victor Hugo

Mistakes are a fact of life.
It is the response to the
error that counts.

Nikki Giovanni

A problem well stated
is a problem half solved.

Charles Kettering

If you aren't happy in one place, chances are you won't
be happy any place.

Ernie Banks

Most of the shadows
of this life are caused by
our standing in our
own sunshine.

Ralph Waldo Emerson

Here's the thing about luck . . . you don't
know if it's good or bad until you have
some perspective.

Alice Hoffman

Perhaps I know best why it is man alone who laughs; he alone suffers so deeply that he had to invent laughter.

Friedrich Nietzsche

The luck will alter and the star will rise.

John Masefield

Men at some time are masters of their fates:
The fault, dear Brutus, is not in our stars,
But in ourselves.

William Shakespeare

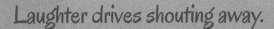

Laughter drives shouting away.

Indra Devi

Hope itself is like a star – not to be seen in the sunshine of prosperity, and only to be discovered in the night of adversity.

Charles H. Spurgeon

Joy and woe are woven fine
A clothing for the soul divine
Under every grief and pine
Runs a joy with silken twine.

William Blake

Sorrow is a part of love and love does not seek
to throw it off.

George Eliot

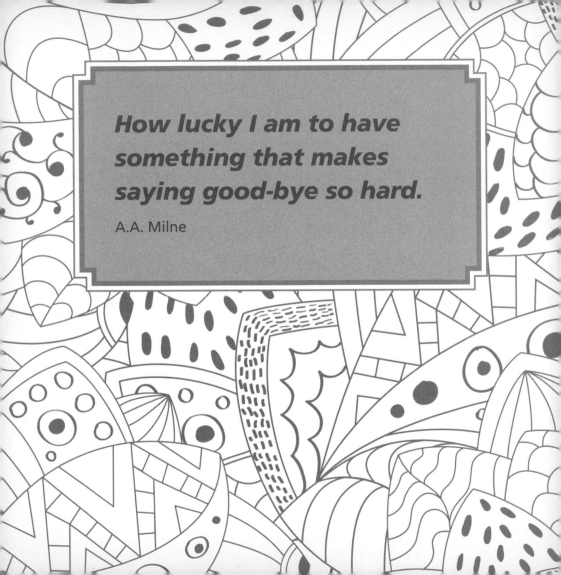

How lucky I am to have something that makes saying good-bye so hard.

A.A. Milne

A man may die,
nations may rise
and fall, but an
idea lives on.

John F. Kennedy

*Laughter is
a tranquillizer with
no side effects.*

Arnold H. Glasow

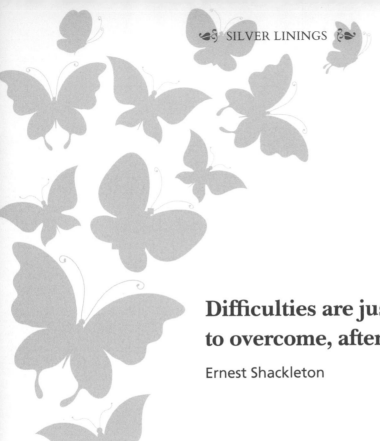

Difficulties are just things to overcome, after all.

Ernest Shackleton

THE POWER OF LAUGHTER

I have great faith in fools
– my friends call it
self-confidence.

Edgar Allan Poe

I like long walks, especially when they are taken by people who annoy me.

Fred Allen

I don't want to achieve immortality through my work. I want to achieve immortality through not dying.

Woody Allen

Happiness is good health and a bad memory.

Ingrid Bergman

The mind is like an umbrella – it only works when it is open.

Sir James Jeans

**Honest criticism
is hard to take,
particularly from
a relative, a friend,
an acquaintance or
a stranger.**

Franklin P. Jones

Bad humour is an evasion of reality; good humour is an acceptance of it.

Malcolm Muggeridge

Some people take no mental exercise apart from jumping to conclusions.

Harold Acton

The person who can bring the spirit of laughter into a room is indeed blessed.

Bennett Cerf

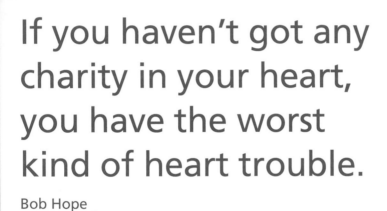

If you haven't got any charity in your heart, you have the worst kind of heart trouble.

Bob Hope

I busted a mirror and got seven years' bad luck, but my lawyer thinks he can get me five.

Steven Wright

My therapist told me the way to achieve true inner peace is to finish what I start. So far, I've finished two bags of M&Ms and a chocolate cake. I feel better already.

Dave Barry

A word to the wise ain't necessary, it is the stupid ones who need all the advice.

Bill Cosby

It is better to offer no excuse than a bad one.

George Washington

The desire to get married is a basic and primal instinct in women. It's followed by another basic and primal instinct: the desire to be single again.

Nora Ephron

It is much more comfortable to be mad and know it, than to be sane and have one's doubts.

G.B. Burgin

People seldom notice old clothes if you wear a big smile.

Lee Mildon

One can never speak enough of the virtues, the dangers, the power of shared laughter.

Françoise Sagan

I have often regretted my speech, never my silence.

Xenocrates

Don't knock the weather; nine-tenths of the people couldn't start a conversation if it didn't change once in a while.

Kin Hubbard

Expecting the world to treat you fairly because you are good is like expecting the bull not to charge because you are a vegetarian.

Dennis Wholey

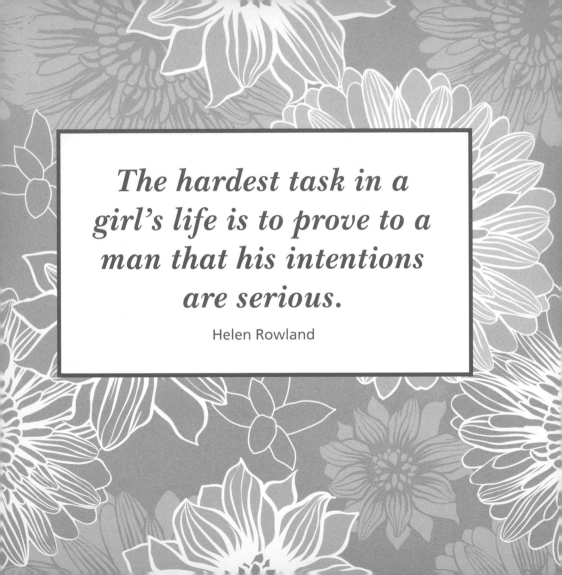

The hardest task in a girl's life is to prove to a man that his intentions are serious.

Helen Rowland

I don't have to look up my family tree, because I know that I'm the sap.

Fred Allen

Reality is whatever refuses to go away when I stop believing in it.

Philip K. Dick

If a mistake is not a stepping stone, it is a mistake.

Eli Siegel

A day without sunshine is like, you know, night.

Steve Martin

Most virtue is a demand for greater seduction.

Natalie Clifford Barney

Lord! What a strange world in which a man cannot remain unique even by taking the trouble to go mad!

G.K. Chesterton

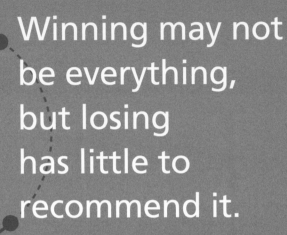

Winning may not
be everything,
but losing
has little to
recommend it.

Dianne Feinstein

If love is the
answer, could you
please rephrase
the question?

Lily Tomlin

Everybody knows how to raise children, except the people who have them.

P.J. O'Rourke

Reason is a very light rider and easily shook off.

Jonathan Swift

In order to keep a true perspective of one's importance, everyone should have a dog that will worship him and a cat that will ignore him.

Dereke Bruce

Drawing on my fine command of the English language, I said nothing.

Robert Benchley

Several excuses are always less convincing than one.

Aldous Huxley

Why do you have to be a nonconformist like everybody else?

James Thurber

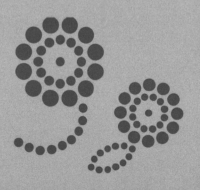

It is the ordinary woman who knows something about love. The gorgeous ones are too busy being gorgeous.

Katharine Hepburn

He who laughs, lasts.

Mary Pettibone Poole

If you are going
through hell,
keep going.

Sir Winston Churchill

What you think is the point is not the point at all but only the beginning of the sharpness.

Flann O'Brien

I have not failed. I've just found 10,000 ways that won't work.

Thomas Edison

A day without laughter is a day wasted.

Charlie Chaplin

Just 'cause you got the monkey off your back doesn't mean the circus has left town.

George Carlin

My friends tell me I have an intimacy problem. But they don't really know me.

Garry Shandling

I don't hate people. I just feel better when they aren't around.

Charles Bukowski

Happiness is having a large, loving, close-knit family in another city.

George Burns

I try to take one day at a time, but sometimes several days attack me at once.

Jennifer Yane

For fast-acting relief, try slowing down.

Lily Tomlin

I guess I just prefer to see the dark side of things. The glass is always half empty. And cracked. And I just cut my lip on it. And chipped a tooth.

Janeane Garofalo

A smile is an inexpensive way to change your looks.

Charles Gordy

It is foolish to tear one's hair in grief, as though sorrow would be made less by baldness.

Cicero

If everything is under control, you are just not going fast enough.

Mario Andretti

Mistrust all enterprises that require new clothes.

E.M. Forster

There is nothing better than a friend, unless it is a friend with chocolate.

Linda Grayson

There's a limit to how many times you can read how great you are and what an inspiration you are, but I'm not there yet.

Randy Pausch

Laughter is the best medicine — unless you're diabetic, then insulin comes pretty high on the list.

Jasper Carrott

A woman is like a tea bag – you never know how strong she is until she gets in hot water.

Eleanor Roosevelt

We are not retreating – we are advancing in another direction.

General Douglas MacArthur

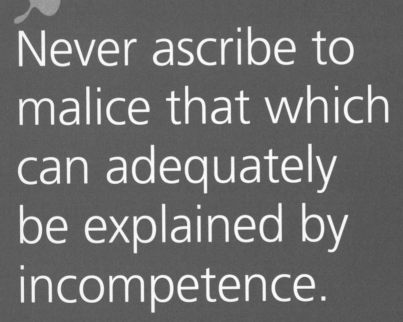

Never ascribe to malice that which can adequately be explained by incompetence.

Napoleon Bonaparte

We learn from history that we learn nothing from history.

George Bernard Shaw

I never make stupid mistakes. Only very, very clever ones.

John Peel

It is the ability to take a joke, not make one, that proves you have a sense of humor.

Max Eastman

Wise men don't need advice. Fools won't take it.

Benjamin Franklin

Good things, when short, are twice as good.

Baltasar Gracián

The way taxes are, you might as well marry for love.

Joe E. Lewis

Whatever women do they must do twice as well as men to be thought half as good. Luckily, this is not difficult.

Charlotte Whitton

There's one thing about baldness, it's neat.

Don Herold

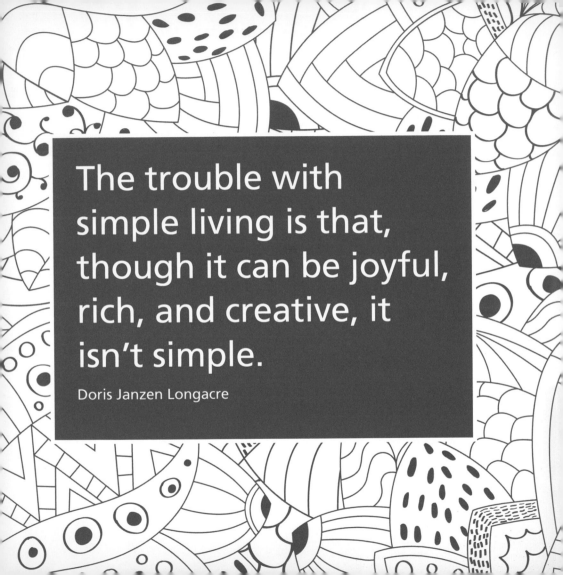

The trouble with simple living is that, though it can be joyful, rich, and creative, it isn't simple.

Doris Janzen Longacre

Even if you're on the right track, you'll get run over if you just sit there.

Will Rogers

A sense of humor is just common sense, dancing.

William James

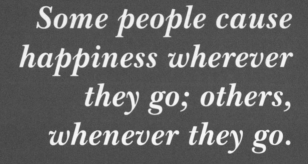

Some people cause happiness wherever they go; others, whenever they go.

Oscar Wilde

We rarely find that people have good sense unless they agree with us.

Emily Dickinson

When I look around me at the men, I feel that God never meant us women to be too particular.

Marie Jenney Howe

Things are going to get
a lot worse before they
get worse.

Lily Tomlin

Imagination was given to man to compensate him for what he is not; a sense of humour to console him for what he is.

Francis Bacon

The fool doth
think he is wise,
but the wise man
knows himself to
be a fool.

William Shakespeare

I don't like to meddle in my private affairs.

Karl Kraus

Humor does not diminish the pain – it makes the space around it get bigger.

Allen Klein

If at first you don't succeed . . . so much for skydiving.

Henry Youngman

I am thankful for laughter, except when milk comes out of my nose.

Woody Allen

Too often, the opportunity knocks, but by the time you push back the chain, push back the bolt, unhook the two locks and shut off the burglar alarm, it's too late.

Rita Coolidge

In Hollywood, we acquire the finest novels in order to smell the leather bindings.

Ernst Lubitsch

Life is just one damned thing after another.

Elbert Hubbard

When I die, I want to go peacefully like my grandfather did – in his sleep. Not yelling and screaming like the passengers in his car.

Bob Monkhouse

Those people
who think they
know everything
are a great
annoyance to
those of us
who do.

Isaac Asimov

Humor is the instinct for taking pain playfully.

Max Eastman

Housework can't kill you, but why take a chance?

Phyllis Diller

If life was fair, Elvis would be alive and all the impersonators would be dead.

Johnny Carson

What I'm looking for is a blessing that's not in disguise.

Kitty O'Neill Collins

People who say, 'Let the chips fall where they may', usually figure they will not be hit by a chip.

Bernard Williams

Show me a woman who doesn't feel guilty and I'll show you a man.

Erica Jong

Too bad that all the people who know how to run the country are busy driving taxicabs and cutting hair.

George Burns

Every man desires to live long, but no man would be old.

Jonathan Swift

What is reality, anyway? Just a collective hunch.

Lily Tomlin

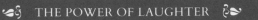

*Failed relationships
can be described
as so much wasted
make-up.*

Marian Keyes

We have no guarantee that the afterlife will be any less
exasperating than this one, have we?

Noel Coward

Most men give advice by the bucket, but take it by the grain.

William R. Alger

Christmas carols always brought tears to my eyes. I also cry at weddings. I should have cried at a couple of my own.

Ethel Merman

A person without a sense of humour is like a wagon without springs. It's jolted by every pebble on the road.

Henry Ward Beecher